The American Poetry Series

Also by Robert Hass

Field Guide

Praise

Robert Hass

The Ecco Press

New York

PRAISE

Some of these poems have been published in the following magazines, to whose editors grateful acknowledgment is made: *Antaeus, Atlantic Monthly, Beatitude, The Berkeley Poetry Review, Boundary 2, Iowa Review, Kenyon Review,* and *Poetry Nation.* "Against Botticelli" first appeared in *The American Poetry Anthology.* "Winter Morning in Charlottesville" appeared in a chapbook of that title printed by the Sceptre Press, Knotting, Bedfordshire, England. Acknowledgment is also made to Yale University Press for permission to reprint "After Chekhov" which has become one of the "Songs to Survive the Summer."

I also want to thank the U.S.–U.K. Exchange Fellowships in the Arts for a grant which allowed me to finish this book.

First published by The Ecco Press in 1979
1 West 30th Street, New York, N.Y. 10001
Published simultaneously in Canada by
Penguin Books Canada Limited
Printed in the United States of America
The Ecco Press logo by Ahmed Yacoubi
Typography by Cynthia Krupat
The publication of this book is partially supported
by a grant from the National Endowment for the Arts

Library of Congress Cataloging in Publication Data
Hass, Robert. / Praise.
  (American poetry series; 17)
  I. Title.
PS3558.A725P7   811'.5'4   78–16016
ISBN 0–912–94661–X (hardbound)
ISBN 0–912–94662–8 (paperback)

To Earlene

Contents

II

I

*We asked the captain what course
of action he proposed to take toward
a beast so large, terrifying, and
unpredictable. He hesitated to
answer, and then said judiciously:
"I think I shall praise it."*

Heroic Simile

When the swordsman fell in Kurosawa's *Seven Samurai*
in the gray rain,
in Cinemascope and the Tokugawa dynasty,
he fell straight as a pine, he fell
as Ajax fell in Homer
in chanted dactyls and the tree was so huge
the woodsman returned for two days
to that lucky place before he was done with the sawing
and on the third day he brought his uncle.

They stacked logs in the resinous air,
hacking the small limbs off,
tying those bundles separately.
The slabs near the root
were quartered and still they were awkwardly large;
the logs from midtree they halved:
ten bundles and four great piles of fragrant wood,
moons and quarter moons and half moons
ridged by the saw's tooth.

The woodsman and the old man his uncle
are standing in midforest
on a floor of pine silt and spring mud.
They have stopped working
because they are tired and because

I have imagined no pack animal
or primitive wagon. They are too canny
to call in neighbors and come home
with a few logs after three days' work.
They are waiting for me to do something
or for the overseer of the Great Lord
to come and arrest them.

How patient they are!
The old man smokes a pipe and spits.
The young man is thinking he would be rich
if he were already rich and had a mule.
Ten days of hauling
and on the seventh day they'll probably
be caught, go home empty-handed
or worse. I don't know
whether they're Japanese or Mycenaean
and there's nothing I can do.
The path from here to that village
is not translated. A hero, dying,
gives off stillness to the air.
A man and a woman walk from the movies
to the house in the silence of separate fidelities.
There are limits to imagination.

Meditation at Lagunitas

All the new thinking is about loss.
In this it resembles all the old thinking.
The idea, for example, that each particular erases
the luminous clarity of a general idea. That the clown-
faced woodpecker probing the dead sculpted trunk
of that black birch is, by his presence,
some tragic falling off from a first world
of undivided light. Or the other notion that,
because there is in this world no one thing
to which the bramble of *blackberry* corresponds,
a word is elegy to what it signifies.
We talked about it late last night and in the voice
of my friend, there was a thin wire of grief, a tone
almost querulous. After a while I understood that,
talking this way, everything dissolves: *justice,
pine, hair, woman, you* and *I.* There was a woman
I made love to and I remembered how, holding
her small shoulders in my hands sometimes,
I felt a violent wonder at her presence
like a thirst for salt, for my childhood river
with its island willows, silly music from the pleasure boat,
muddy places where we caught the little orange-silver fish
called *pumpkinseed.* It hardly had to do with her.
Longing, we say, because desire is full

of endless distances. I must have been the same to her.
But I remember so much, the way her hands dismantled bread,
the thing her father said that hurt her, what
she dreamed. There are moments when the body is as numinous
as words, days that are the good flesh continuing.
Such tenderness, those afternoons and evenings,
saying *blackberry, blackberry, blackberry.*

Sunrise

Ah, love, this is fear. This is fear and syllables
and the beginnings of beauty. We have walked the city,
a flayed animal signifying death, a hybrid god
who sings in the desolation of filth and money
a song the heart is heavy to receive. We mourn
otherwise. Otherwise the ranked monochromes,
the death-teeth of that horizon, survive us
as we survive pleasure. What a small hope.
What a fierce small privacy of consolation.
What a dazzle of petals for the poor meat.

Blind, with eyes like stars, like astral flowers,
from the purblind mating sickness of the beasts
we rise, trout-shaken, in the gaping air,
in terror, the scarlet sun-flash
leaping from the pond's imagination
of a deadly sea. Fish, mole,
we are the small stunned creatures
inside these human resurrections, the nights
the city praises and defiles. From there we all
walk slowly to the sea gathering scales
from the cowled whisper of the waves,
the mensural polyphony. Small stars,
and blind the hunger under sun,

we turn to each other and turn to each other
in the mother air of what we want.

That is why blind Orpheus praises love
and why love gouges out our eyes
and why all lovers smell their way to Dover.
That is why innocence has so much to account for,
why Venus appears least saintly in the attitudes of shame.
This is lost children and the deep sweetness of the pulp,
a blue thrumming at the formed bone, river,
flame, quicksilver. It is not the fire
we hunger for and not the ash. It is the still hour,
a deer come slowly to the creek at dusk,
the table set for abstinence, windows
full of flowers like summer in the provinces
vanishing when the moon's half-face pallor
rises on the dark flax line of hills.

The Yellow Bicycle

The woman I love is greedy,
but she refuses greed.
She walks so straightly.
When I ask her what she wants,
she says, "A yellow bicycle."

•

Sun, sunflower,
coltsfoot on the roadside,
a goldfinch, the sign
that says Yield, her hair,
cat's eyes, his hunger
and a yellow bicycle.

•

Once, when they had made love in the middle of the night and
it was very sweet, they decided they were hungry, so they got up,
got dressed, and drove downtown to an all-night donut shop.
Chicano kids lounged outside, a few drunks, and one black man
selling dope. Just at the entrance there was an old woman in a
thin floral print dress. She was barefoot. Her face was covered
with sores and dry peeling skin. The sores looked like raisins and
her skin was the dry yellow of a parchment lampshade ravaged by
light and tossed away. They thought she must have been hungry

and, coming out again with a white paper bag full of hot rolls, they stopped to offer her one. She looked at them out of her small eyes, bewildered, and shook her head for a little while, and said very kindly, "No."

•

Her song to the yellow bicycle:
The boats on the bay
have nothing on you,   .
my swan, my sleek one!

Against Botticelli

1

In the life we lead together every paradise is lost.
Nothing could be easier: summer gathers new leaves
to casual darkness. So few things we need to know.
And the old wisdoms shudder in us and grow slack.
Like renunciation. Like the melancholy beauty
of giving it all up. Like walking steadfast
in the rhythms, winter light and summer dark.
And the time for cutting furrows and the dance.
Mad seed. Death waits it out. It waits us out,
the sleek incandescent saints, earthly and prayerful.
In our modesty. In our shamefast and steady attention
to the ceremony, its preparation, the formal hovering
of pleasure which falls like the rain we pray not to get
and are glad for and drown in. Or spray of that sea,
irised: otters in the tide lash, in the kelp-drench,
mammal warmth and the inhuman element. Ah, that is the secret.
That she is an otter, that Botticelli saw her so.
That we are not otters and are not in the painting
by Botticelli. We are not even in the painting by Bosch
where the people are standing around looking at the frame
of the Botticelli painting and when Love arrives, they throw up.
Or the Goya painting of the sad ones, angular and shriven,

who watch the Bosch and feel very compassionate
but hurt each other often and inefficiently. We are not in any
      painting.
If we do it at all, we will be like the old Russians.
We'll walk down through scrub oak to the sea
and where the seals lie preening on the beach
we will look at each other steadily
and butcher them and skin them.

2

The myth they chose was the constant lovers.
The theme was richness over time.
It is a difficult story and the wise never choose it
because it requires a long performance
and because there is nothing, by definition, between the acts.
It is different in kind from a man and the pale woman
he fucks in the ass underneath the stars
because it is summer and they are full of longing
and sick of birth. They burn coolly
like phosphorus, and the thing need be done
only once. Like the sacking of Troy
it survives in imagination,
in the longing brought perfectly to closing,

11

the woman's white hands opening, opening,
and the man churning inside her, thrashing there.
And light travels as if all the stars they were under
exploded centuries ago and they are resting now, glowing.
The woman thinks what she is feeling is like the dark
and utterly complete. The man is past sadness,
though his eyes are wet. He is learning about gratitude,
how final it is, as if the grace in Botticelli's *Primavera*,
the one with sad eyes who represents pleasure,
had a canvas to herself, entirely to herself.

Like Three Fair Branches
from One Root Deriv'd

I am outside a door and inside
the words do not fumble
as I fumble saying this.
It is the same in the dream
where I touch you. Notice
in this poem the thinning out
of particulars. The gate
with the three snakes is burning,
symbolically, which doesn't mean
the flames can't hurt you.
Now it is the pubic arch instead
and smells of oils and driftwood,
of our bodies working very hard
at pleasure but they are not
thinking about us. Bless them,
it is not a small thing to be
happily occupied, go by them
on tiptoe. Now the gate is marble
and the snakes are graces.
You are the figure in the center.
On the left you are going away
from yourself. On the right
you are coming back. Meanwhile
we are passing through the gate

with everything we love. We go
as fire, as flesh, as marble.
Sometimes it is good and sometimes
it is dangerous like the ignorance
of particulars, but our words are clear
and our movements give off light.

Transparent Garments

Because it is neither easy nor difficult,
because the outer dark is not passport
nor is the inner dark, the horror
held in memory as talisman. Not to go in
stupidly holding out dark as some
wrong promise of fidelity, but to go in
as one can, empty or worshipping.
White, as a proposition. Not leprous
by easy association nor painfully radiant.
Or maybe that, yes, maybe painfully.
To go into that. As: I am walking in the city
and there is the whiteness of the houses,
little cubes of it bleaching in the sunlight,
luminous with attritions of light, the failure
of matter in the steadiness of light,
a purification, not burning away,
nothing so violent, something clearer
that stings and stings and is then
past pain or this slow levitation of joy.
And to emerge, where the juniper
is simply juniper and there is the smell
of new shingle, a power saw outside
and inside a woman in the bath,
a scent of lemon and a drift of song,

a heartfelt imitation of Bessie Smith.
The given, as in given up
or given out, as in testimony.

The Image

The child brought blue clay from the creek
and the woman made two figures: a lady and a deer.
At that season deer came down from the mountain
and fed quietly in the redwood canyons.
The woman and the child regarded the figure of the lady,
the crude roundnesses, the grace, the coloring like shadow.
They were not sure where she came from,
except the child's fetching and the woman's hands
and the lead-blue clay of the creek
where the deer sometimes showed themselves at sundown.

The Feast

The lovers loitered on the deck talking,
the men who were with men and the men who were with new
    women,
a little shrill and electric, and the wifely women
who had repose and beautifully lined faces
and coppery skin. She had taken the turkey from the oven
and her friends were talking on the deck
in the steady sunshine. She imagined them
drifting toward the food, in small groups, finishing
sentences, lifting a pickle or a sliver of turkey,
nibbling a little with unconscious pleasure. And
she imagined setting it out artfully, the white meat,
the breads, antipasto, the mushrooms and salad
arranged down the oak counter cleanly, and how they all came
as in a dance when she called them. She carved meat
and then she was crying. Then she was in darkness
crying. She didn't know what she wanted.

The Pure Ones

Roads to the north of here are dry.
First red buds prick out the lethal spring
and corncrakes, swarming, lower in clouds
above the fields from Paris to Béziers.
This is God's harvest: the village boy
whose tongue was sliced in two,
the village crones slashing cartilage
at the knees to crawl to Carcassonne.
—If the world were not evil in itself,
the blessed one said, then every choice
would not constitute a loss.
This sickness of this age is flesh,
he said. Therefore we build with stone.
The dead with their black lips are heaped
on one another, intimate as lovers.

The Garden of Delight

The floor hurts so much it whines
whichever way they step,
as if it had learned the trick
of suffering.
Poor floor.
This is the garden of delight,
a man pointing at a woman
and a bird perched
on a cylinder of crystal
watching. She has a stopper
in her mouth or the paint
has blistered, long ago, just there.
He looks worried, but not terrified,
not terrified, and he doesn't move.
It's an advantage of paintings.
You don't have to.
I used to name the flowers—
beard tongue, stone crop,
pearly everlasting.

Santa Lucia

I

Art & love: he camps outside my door,
innocent, carnivorous. As if desire
were actually a flute, as if the little song
transcend, transcend could get you anywhere.
He brings me wine; he believes in the arts
and uses them for beauty. He brings me
vinegar in small earthen pots, postcards
of the hillsides by Cézanne desire has left
alone, empty farms in August and the vague
tall chestnut trees at Jas de Bouffan, fetal
sandstone rifted with mica from the beach.
He brings his body, wolfish, frail,
all brown for summer like croissant crusts
at La Seine in the Marina, the bellies
of pelicans I watched among white dunes
under Pico Blanco on the Big Sur coast.
It sickens me, this glut & desperation.

II

Walking the Five Springs trail, I tried to think.
Dead-nettle, thimbleberry. The fog heaved in

between the pines, violet sparrows made curves
like bodies in the ruined air. *All women
are masochists.* I was so young, believing
every word they said. *Dürer is second-rate.*
Dürer's Eve feeds her apple to the snake;
snaky tresses, cat at her feet, at Adam's foot
a mouse. Male fear, male eyes and art. The art
of love, the eyes I use to see myself
in love. Ingres, pillows. I think the erotic
is not sexual, only when you're lucky.
That's where the path forks. It's not the riddle
of desire that interests me; it is the riddle
of good hands, chervil in a windowbox,
the white pages of a book, someone says
I'm tired, someone turning on the light.

III

Streaked in the window, the city wavers
but the sky is empty, clean. Emptiness
is strict; that pleases me. I do cry out.
Like everyone else, I thrash, am splayed.
Oh, oh, oh, oh. Eyes full of wonder.
Guernica. Ulysses on the beach. I see

my body is his prayer. I see my body.
Walking in the galleries at the Louvre,
I was, each moment, naked & possessed.
Tourists gorged on goosenecked Florentine girls
by Pollaiuolo. He sees me like a painter.
I hear his words for me: white, gold.
I'd rather walk the city in the rain.
Dog shit, traffic accidents. Whatever god
there is dismembered in his Chevy.
A different order of religious awe:
agony & meat, everything plain afterwards.

IV

Santa Lucia: eyes jellied on a plate.
The thrust of serpentine was almost green
all through the mountains where the rock cropped out.
I liked sundowns, dusks smelling of madrone,
the wildflowers, which were not beautiful,
fierce little wills rooting in the yellow
grass year after year, thirst in the roots,
mineral. They have intelligence
of hunger. Poppies lean to the morning sun,
lupine grows thick in the rockface, self-heal

at creekside. He wants to fuck. Sweet word.
All suction. I want less. Not that I fear
the huge dark of sex, the sharp sweet light,
light if it were water raveling, rancor,
tenderness like rain. What I want happens
not when the deer freezes in the shade
and looks at you and you hold very still
and meet her gaze but in the moment after
when she flicks her ears & starts to feed again.

To a Reader

I've watched memory wound you.
I felt nothing but envy.
Having slept in wet meadows,
I was not through desiring.
Imagine January and the beach,
a bleached sky, gulls. And
look seaward: what is not there
is there, isn't it, the huge
bird of the first light
arched above first waters
beyond our touching or intention
or the reasonable shore.

The Origin of Cities

She is first seen dancing which is a figure
not for art or prayer or the arousal of desire
but for action simply; her breastband is copper,
her crown imitates the city walls. Though she draws us
to her, like a harbor or a rivermouth she sends us away.
A figure of the outward. So the old men grown lazy
in patrician ways lay out cash for adventures.
Imagining a rich return, they buy futures
and their slaves haunt the waterfront for news of ships.
The young come from the villages dreaming.
Pleasure and power draw them. They are employed
to make inventories and grow very clever,
multiplying in their heads, deft at the use of letters.
When they are bored, they write down old songs from the villages,
and the cleverest make new songs in the old forms
describing the pleasures of the city, their mistresses,
old shepherds and simpler times. And the temple
where the farmer grandfathers of the great merchants worshipped,
the dim temple across from the marketplace
which was once a stone altar in a clearing in the forest,
where the nightwatch pisses now against a column in the
        moonlight,
is holy to them; the wheat mother their goddess of sweaty sheets,
of what is left in the air when that glimpsed beauty

turns the corner, of love's punishment and the wracking
of desire. They make songs about that. They tell
stories of heroes and brilliant lust among the gods.
These are amusements. She dances, the ships go forth,
slaves and peasants labor in the fields, maimed soldiers
ape monkeys for coins outside the wineshops,
the craftsmen work in bronze and gold, accounts
are kept carefully, what goes out, what returns.

Winter Morning in Charlottesville

Lead skies
and gothic traceries of poplar.
In the sacrament of winter
Savonarola raged against the carnal word.

Inside the prism of that eloquence
even Botticelli renounced the bestial gods
and beauty.
          Florentine vanity
gathers in the dogwood buds.
How sexual
this morning is the otherwise
quite plain
white-crowned sparrow's
plumed head!
         By a natural
selection, the word
originates its species,
             the blood flowers,
republics scrawl their hurried declarations
& small birds scavenge
         in the chaste late winter grass.

Old Dominion

The shadows of late afternoon and the odors
of honeysuckle are a congruent sadness.
Everything is easy but wrong. I am walking
across thick lawns under maples in borrowed tennis whites.
It is like the photographs of Randall Jarrell
I stared at on the backs of books in college.
He looked so sad and relaxed in the pictures.
He was translating Chekhov and wore tennis whites.
It puzzled me that in his art, like Chekhov's,
everyone was lost, that the main chance was never seized
because it is only there as a thing to be dreamed of
or because someone somewhere had set the old words
to the old tune: we live by habit and it doesn't hurt.
Now the *thwack* . . . *thwack* of tennis balls being hit
reaches me and it is the first sound of an ax
in the cherry orchard or the sound of machine guns
where the young terrorists are exploding
among poor people on the streets of Los Angeles.
I begin making resolutions: to take risks, not to stay
in the south, to somehow do honor to Randall Jarrell,
never to kill myself. Through the oaks I see the courts,
the nets, the painted boundaries, and the people in tennis
whites who look so graceful from this distance.

Monticello

Snow is falling
on the age of reason, on Tom Jefferson's
little hill & on the age of sensibility.

Jane Austen isn't walking in the park,
she considers that this gray crust
of an horizon will not do;
she is by the fire, reading William Cowper,
and Jefferson, if he isn't dead,
has gone down to K-Mart
to browse among the gadgets:
pulleys, levers, the separation of powers.

I try to think of history: the mammoth
jawbone in the entry hall,
Napoleon in marble,
Meriwether Lewis dead at Grinder's Trace.

I don't want the powers separated,
one wing for Governor Randolph when he comes,
the other wing for love,
private places
in the public weal
that ache against the teeth like ice.

Outside this monument, the snow
catches, star-shaped,
in the vaginal leaves of old magnolias.

Emblems of a Prior Order

(For Louise)

Patient cultivation,
as the white petals of
the climbing rose

were to some man
a lifetime's careful work,
the mess of petals

on the lawn was bred
to fall there as a dog
is bred to stand—

gardens are a history
of art, this fin-de-siècle
flower & Dobermann's

pinscher, all deadly
sleekness in the neighbor's
yard, were born, *brennende*

liebe, under the lindens
that bear the morning
toward us on a silver tray.

Weed

Horse is Lorca's word, fierce as wind,
or melancholy, gorgeous, Andalusian:
 white horse grazing near the river dust;
and parsnip is hopeless,
 second cousin to the rhubarb
which is already second cousin
 to an apple pie. Marrying the words
to the coarse white umbels sprouting
 on the first of May is history
but conveys nothing; it is not the veined
 body of Queen Anne's lace
I found, bored, in a spring classroom
 from which I walked hands tingling
for the breasts that are meadows in New Jersey
 in 1933; it is thick, shaggier, and the name
is absurd. It speaks of durable
 unimaginative pleasures: reading Balzac,
fixing the window sash, rising
 to a clean kitchen, the fact
that the car starts & driving to work
 through hills where the roadside thickens
with the green ungainly stalks,
 the bracts and bright white flowerets
  of horse-parsnips.

Child Naming Flowers

When old crones wandered in the woods,
I was the hero on the hill
in clear sunlight.

Death's hounds feared me.

Smell of wild fennel,
high loft of sweet fruit high in the branches
of the flowering plum.

Then I am cast down
into the terror of childhood,
into the mirror and the greasy knives,
the dark
woodpile under the fig trees
in the dark.
        It is only
the malice of voices, the old horror
that is nothing, parents
quarreling, somebody
drunk.

I don't know how we survive it.
On this sunny morning

in my life as an adult, I am looking
at one clear pure peach
in a painting by Georgia O'Keeffe.
It is all the fullness that there is
in light. A towhee scratches in the leaves
outside my open door.
He always does.

A moment ago I felt so sick
and so cold
I could hardly move.

Picking Blackberries with a Friend
Who Has Been Reading Jacques Lacan

August is dust here. Drought
stuns the road,
but juice gathers in the berries.

We pick them in the hot
slow-motion of midmorning.
Charlie is exclaiming:

for him it is twenty years ago
and raspberries and Vermont.
We have stopped talking

about *L'Histoire de la vérité*,
about subject and object
and the mediation of desire.

Our ears are stoppered
in the bee-hum. And Charlie,
laughing wonderfully,

beard stained purple
by the word *juice*,
goes to get a bigger pot.

The Beginning of September

I

The child is looking in the mirror.
His head falls to one side, his shoulders slump.
He is practicing sadness.

II

He didn't think she ought to
and she thought she should.

III

In the summer
peaches the color of sunrise

In the fall
plums the color of dusk

IV

Each thing moves its own way
in the wind. Bamboo flickers,
the plum tree waves, and the loquat
is shaken.

V

The dangers are everywhere. Auxiliary verbs, fishbones, a fine carelessness. No one really likes the odor of geraniums, not the woman who dreams of sunlight and is always late for work nor the man who would be happy in altered circumstances. Words are abstract, but *words are abstract* is a dance, car crash, heart's delight. It's the design dumb hunger has upon the world. Nothing is severed on hot mornings when the deer nibble flowerheads in a simmer of bay leaves. Somewhere in the summer dusk is the sound of children setting the table. That is mastery: spoon, knife, folded napkin, fork; glasses all around. The place for the plate is wholly imagined. Mother sits here and father sits there and this is your place and this is mine. A good story compels you like sexual hunger but the pace is more leisurely. And there are always melons.

VI

little mother
little dragonfly quickness of summer mornings
this is a prayer
this is the body dressed in its own warmth
at the change of seasons

VII

There are not always melons
There are always stories

VIII

Chester found a dozen copies of his first novel in a used book-store and took them to the counter. The owner said, "You can't have them all," so Chester kept five. The owner said, "That'll be a hundred and twelve dollars." Chester said, "What?" and the guy said, "They're first editions, mac, twenty bucks apiece." And so Chester said, "Why are you charging me a hundred and twelve dollars?" The guy said, "Three of them are autographed." Chester said, "Look, I wrote this book." The guy said, "All right, a hundred. I won't charge you for the autographs."

IX

The insides of peaches
are the color of sunrise

The outsides of plums
are the color of dusk

X

Here are some things to pray to in San Francisco: the bay, the
mountain, the goddess of the city; remembering, forgetting, sud-
den pleasure, loss; sunrise and sunset; salt; the tutelary gods of
Chinese, Japanese, Russian, Basque, French, Italian and Mexi-
can cooking; the solitude of coffee houses and museums; the
virgin, mother and widow moons; hilliness, vistas; John McLaren;
Saint Francis; the Mother of Sorrows; the rhythm of any life still
whole through three generations; wine, especially zinfandel be-
cause from that Hungarian vine-slip came first a native wine not
resinous and sugar-heavy; the sourdough mother, true yeast and
beginning; all fish and fisherman at the turning of the tide; the
turning of the tide; eelgrass, oldest inhabitant; fog; seagulls;
Joseph Worcester; plum blossoms; warm days in January . . .

XI

She thought it was a good idea.
He had his doubts.

XII

ripe blackberries

XIII

She said: reside, reside
and he said, gored heart
She said: sunlight, cypress
he said, idiot children
nibbling arsenic in flaking paint
she said: a small pool of semen
translucent on my belly
he said maybe he said
maybe

XIV

the sayings of my grandmother:
they're the kind of people
who let blackberries rot on the vine

XV

The child approaches the mirror very fast
then stops
and watches himself
gravely.

XVI

So summer gives over—
white to the color of straw
dove gray to slate blue
    burnishings
a little rain
a little light on the water

Not Going to New York: A Letter

Dear Dan—
          This is a letter of apology, unrhymed.
Rhyme belongs to the dazzling couplets of arrival.
Survival is the art around here. It rhymes by accident
with the rhythm of days which arrive like crows in a field
of stubble corn in upstate New York in February.
In upstate New York in February thaws hardened the heart
against the wish for spring. There was not one thing
in the barren meadows not muddy and raw-fleshed.
At night I dreamed of small black snakes with orange markings
disappearing down their holes, of being lost in the hemlocks
and coming to a clearing of wild strawberry, sunlight,
abandoned apple trees. At night it was mild noon in a clearing.
Nothing arrived. This was a place left to flower
in the plain cruelty of light. Mornings the sky was opal.
The windows faced east and a furred snow reassumed the pines
but arrived only mottled in the fields so that its flesh
was my grandmother's in the kitchen of the house
on Jackson Street, and she was crying. I was a good boy.
She held me so tight when she said that, smelling like sleep
rotting if sleep rots, that I always knew how death would come
to get me and the soft folds of her quivery white neck
were what I saw, so that sometimes on an airplane I look down
to snow covering the arroyos on the east side of the Sierra

and it's grandmother's flesh and I look away. In the house
on Jackson Street, I am the figure against the wall
in Bonnard's *The Breakfast Room*. The light is terrible. It is
wishes that are fat dogs, already sated, snuffling
at the heart in dreams. The table linen is so crisp
it puts an end to fantasies of rectitude, clean hands, high art
and the blue beside the white in the striping is the color
of the river Loire when you read about it in old books
and dreamed of provincial breakfasts, the sun the color
of bread crust and the fruit icy cold and there was no
terrified figure dwarf-like and correct, disappearing
off the edge of Bonnard's *The Breakfast Room*. It was not
grandmother weeping in the breakfast room or the first thaw
dream of beautiful small snakes slithering down holes.
In this life that is not dreams but my life
the clouds above the bay are massing toward December
and gulls hover in the storm-pearled air and the last
of last season's cedar spits and kindles on the fire.
Summer dries us out with golden light, so winter
is a kind of spring here—wet trees, a reptile odor
in the earth, mild greening—and the seasonal myths
lie across one another in the quick darkening of days.
Kristin and Luke are bent to a puzzle, some allegory
of the quattrocento cut in a thousand small uneven pieces

which, on the floor, they recompose with rapt,
leisurely attention. Kristin asks, searching
for a piece round at one end, fluted at the other,
"Do you know what a shepherd is?" and Luke, looking for
a square edge with a sprig of Italian olive in it,
makes a guess. "Somebody who hurts sheep."
My grandmother was not so old. She was my mother's mother;
I think, the night before, my father must have told her
we were going to move. She held me weeping, probably,
because she felt she was about to lose her daughter.
We only buried her this year. In the genteel hotel
on Leavenworth that looked across a mile of human misery
to the bay, she smoked regally, complained about her teeth.
Luke watched her wide-eyed, with a mingled look of wonder
and religious dread she seemed so old. And once,
when he reached up involuntarily to touch her withered cheek,
she looked at him awhile and patted his cheek back and winked
and said to me, askance: "Old age ain't for sissies."
This has nothing to do with the odd terror in my memory.
It only explains it—the way this early winter weather
makes life seem more commonplace and—at a certain angle—
more intense. It is not poetry where decay and a created
radiance lie hidden inside words the way that memory
folds them into living. "O Westmoreland thou art a summer bird

that ever in the haunch of winter sings the lifting up of day."
Pasternak translated those lines. I imagine Russian summer,
the smell of jasmine drifting toward the porch. I would like
to get on a plane, but I would also like to sit on the porch
and watch one shrink to the hovering of gulls and glint
in the distance, circle east toward snow and disappear.
He would have noticed the articles as a native speaker wouldn't:
a bird, *the* haunch; and understood a little what persists
when, eyes half-closed, lattice-shadow on his face,
he murmured the phrase in the dark vowels of his mother tongue.

II

It's funny, isn't it, Karamazov,
all this grief and pancakes afterwards . . .

Songs to Survive the Summer

These are the dog days,
unvaried
except by accident,

mist rising from soaked lawns,
gone world, everything
rises and dissolves in air,

whatever it is would
clear the air
dissolves in air and the knot

of days unties
invisibly like a shoelace.
The gray-eyed child

who said to my child: "Let's play
in my yard. It's OK,
my mother's dead."

•

Under the loquat tree.
It's almost a song,
the echo of a song:

on the bat's back I fly
merrily toward summer
or at high noon

in the outfield clover
guzzling Orange Crush,
time endless, examining

a wooden coin I'd carried
all through summer
without knowing it.

The coin was grandpa's joke,
carved from live oak,
Indian side and buffalo side.

His eyes lustered with a mirth
so deep and rich he never
laughed, as if it were a cosmic

secret that we shared.
I never understood; it married
in my mind with summer. Don't

take any wooden nickels,
kid, and gave me one
under the loquat tree.

•

The squalor of mind
is formlessness,
informis,

the Romans said of ugliness,
it has no form,
a man's misery, bleached skies,

the war between desire
and dailiness. I thought
this morning of Wallace Stevens

walking equably to work
and of a morning two Julys ago
on Chestnut Ridge, wandering

down the hill when one
rusty elm leaf, earth-
skin peeling, wafted

by me on the wind.
My body groaned toward fall
and preternaturally

a heron lifted from the pond.
I even thought I heard
the ruffle of the wings

three hundred yards below me
rising from the reeds.
Death is the mother of beauty

and that clean-shaven man
smelling of lotion,
lint-free, walking

toward his work, a
pure exclusive music
in his mind.

•

The mother of the neighbor
child was thirty-one,
died, at Sunday breakfast,

of a swelling in the throat.
On a toy loom
she taught my daughter

how to weave. My daughter
was her friend
and now she cannot sleep

for nighttime sirens,
sure that every wail
is someone dead.

Should I whisper in her ear,
death is the mother
of beauty? Wooden

nickels, kid? It's all in
shapeliness, give your
fears a shape?

.

In fact, we hide together
in her books.
Prairie farms, the heron

knows the way, old
country songs, herbal magic,
recipes for soup,

tales of spindly orphan
girls who find
the golden key, the

darkness at the center
of the leafy wood.
And when she finally sleeps

I try out Chekhov's
tenderness to see
what it can save.

•

Maryushka the beekeeper's
widow,
though three years mad,

writes daily letters
to her son. Semyon tran-
scribes them. The pages

are smudged by his hands,
stained with
the dregs of tea:

"My dearest Vanushka,
Sofia Agrippina's ill
again. The master

asks for you. Wood
is dear. The cold
is early. Poor

Sofia Agrippina!
The foreign doctor
gave her salts

but Semyon says her icon
candle guttered
St. John's eve. I am afraid,

Vanya. When she's ill,
the master likes to have
your sister flogged.

54

She means no harm.
The rye is gray
this time of year.

When it is bad, Vanya,
I go into the night
and the night eats me."

    •

The haiku comes
in threes
with the virtues of brevity:

> *What a strange thing!*
> *To be alive*
> *beneath plum blossoms.*

The black-headed
Steller's jay is squawking
in our plum.

Thief! Thief!
A hard, indifferent bird,
he'd snatch your life.

•

The love of books
is for children
who glimpse in them

a life to come, but
I have come
to that life and

feel uneasy
with the love of books.
This is my life,

time islanded
in poems of dwindled time.
There is no other world.

•

But I have seen it twice.
In the Palo Alto marsh
sea birds rose in early light

and took me with them.
Another time, dreaming,
river birds lifted me,

swans, small angelic terns,
and an old woman in a shawl
dying by a dying lake

whose life raised men
from the dead
in another country.

•

Thick nights, and nothing
lets us rest. In the heat
of mid-July our lust

is nothing. We swell
and thicken. Slippery,
purgatorial, our sexes

will not give us up.
Exhausted after hours
and not undone,

we crave cold marrow
from the tiny bones that
moonlight scatters

on our skin. Always
morning arrives,
the stunned days,

faceless, droning
in the juice of rotten quince,
the flies, the heat.

•

Tears, silence.
The edified generations
eat me, Maryushka.

I tell them
pain is form and
almost persuade

myself. They are not
listening. Why
should they? Who

cannot save me any more
than I, weeping
over *Great Russian Short*

Stories in summer,
under the fattened figs,
saved you. Besides

it is winter there.
They are trying out
a new recipe for onion soup.

•

Use a heavy-bottomed
three- or four-quart pan.
Thinly slice six large

yellow onions and sauté
in olive oil and butter
until limp. Pour in

beef broth. Simmer
thirty minutes,
add red port and bake

for half an hour. Then
sprinkle half a cup
of diced Gruyère and cover

with an even layer
of toasted bread and
shredded Samsoe. Dribble

melted butter on the top
and bake until the cheese
has bubbled gold.

Surround yourself with friends.
Huddle in a warm place.
Ladle. Eat.

•

Weave and cry.
Child, every other siren
is a death;

the rest are for speeding.
Look how comically the jay's
black head emerges

from a swath of copper leaves.
Half the terror
is the fact that,

in our time, speed saves us,
a whine we've traded
for the hopeless patience

of the village bell
which tolled in threes:
weave and cry and weave.

●

Wilhelm Steller, form's
hero, made
a healing broth.

He sailed with Bering
and the crew despised him,
a mean impatient man

born low enough
to hate the lower class.
For two years

he'd connived to join
the expedition and put
his name to all the beasts

and flowers of the north.
Now Bering sick,
the crew half-mad with scurvy,

no one would let him
go ashore. Panic,
the maps were useless,

the summer weather almost gone.
He said, there are herbs
that can cure you,

I can save you all. He didn't
give a damn about them
and they knew it. For two years

he'd prepared. Bering listened.
Asleep in his bunk, he'd
seen death writing in the log.

On the island while
the sailors searched for water
Steller gathered herbs

and looking up
he saw the blue, black-crested
bird, shrilling in a pine.

His mind flipped to
Berlin, the library, a glimpse
he'd had at Audubon,

a blue-gray crested bird
exactly like the one
that squawked at him, a

Carolina jay, unlike
any European bird; he knew
then where they were,

America, we're saved.
No one believed him or,
sick for home, he didn't care

what wilderness
it was. They set sail
west. Bering died.

Steller's jay, by which
I found Alaska.
He wrote it in his book.

.

Saved no one. Still,
walking in the redwoods
I hear the cry

thief, thief and
think of Wilhelm Steller;
in my dream we

are all saved. Camping
on a clement shore
in early fall, a strange land.

We feast most delicately.
The swans are stuffed with grapes,
the turkey with walnut

and chestnut and wild plum.
The river is our music: *unalaska*
(to make bread from acorns

we leach the tannic acid out—
this music, child,
and more, much more!)

.

When I was just
your age, the war was over
and we moved.

An Okie family lived
next door to our new
country house. That summer

Quincy Phipps was saved.
The next his house became
an unofficial Pentecostal church.

Summer nights: hidden
in the garden I ate figs,
watched where the knobby limbs

rose up and flicked
against the windows where
they were. *O Je-sus.*

Kissed and put to bed,
I slipped from the window
to the eaves and nestled

by the loquat tree.
The fruit was yellow-brown
in daylight; under the moon

pale clusters hung
like other moons, *O
Je-sus*, and I picked them;

the fat juices
dribbling down my chin,
I sucked and listened.

Men groaned. The women
sobbed and moaned, a
long unsteady belly-deep

bewildering sound, half
pleasure and half pain
that ended sometimes

in a croon, a broken song:
O Je-sus,
Je-sus.

•

That is what I have
to give you, child, stories,
songs, loquat seeds,

curiously shaped; they
are the frailest stay against
our fears. Death

in the sweetness, in the bitter
and the sour, death
in the salt, your tears,

this summer ripe and overripe.
It is a taste in the mouth,
child. We are the song

death takes its own time
singing. It calls us
as I call you *child*

to calm myself. It is every
thing touched casually,
lovers, the images

of saviors, books, the coin
I carried in my pocket
till it shone, it is

all things lustered
by the steady thoughtlessness
of human use.

Robert Hass lives with his wife and three children
in Berkeley, California. He grew up in San Francisco
and attended St. Mary's College and Stanford University.
His first book, *Field Guide,* won the Yale Series of
Younger Poets Award in 1973.